CONTENTS

HOW TO USE THIS BOOK

There are thousands of different plants and animals to be found in and around the ponds and lakes of the British Isles and other European countries. This book is an identification guide to some of the most common and to a selection of the rarer ones.

will be very rare in the British Isles, but you can keep an eye out for them when you visit other European countries.

AREAS COVERED
The green area on this map shows the countries covered by this book. Some animals and plants

SPOTTER'S GUIDE TO
PONDS & LAKES

Written by Anthony Wotton

Illustrated by John Barber, Trevor Boyer, Hilary Burn,
Tim Hayward, Aziz Khan, Alan Male, Andy Martin,
Annabel Milne, Peter Stebbing, David Palmer,
Julie Piper, Chris Shields and Phil Weare

Edited by Philippa Wingate and Felicity Mansfield
Series editor: Philippa Wingate
Designed by Cecilia Bonilla
Cover and series designer: Laura Fearn
Expert consultant: Margaret Rostron

The publisher would like to thank the following organizations
for the photographs: p.1 © Wolfgang Kaehler/Corbis;
p.2/3 © Peter Johnson/Corbis; p.4/5 © Gordon
Whitten/Corbis; p.8/9 © Gunter Marx/Corbis;
backgrounds: p.10-64 Digital Vision.

First published in 2000 by Usborne Publishing Ltd.,
Usborne House, 83-85 Saffron Hill, London, EC1N 8RT,
England. www.usborne.com
Copyright © 2000, 1986, 1980 Usborne Publishing Ltd.
The name Usborne and the device 🐝 are Trade Marks of
Usborne Publishing Ltd.

Printed in Spain

Some of the more difficult words in this book are explained on pages 56-57.

IDENTIFICATION
Each kind of animal or plant is called a "species".

To help you identify them, the book contains descriptions and pictures. A description may include information about where you will find an animal or plant and how big it is. Here is an example.

Picture of the species

◄ KINGFISHER
Usually lives near running water, but may be seen by ponds or lakes. Nests in a hole tunnelled in soft earth in the bank. Dives from a perch to catch fishes. 17cm long.

Circle to tick once you have spotted this species.

Size in metres, centimetres or millimetres (see page 10).

WHEN AND WHERE TO SPOT

The best time to go spotting is in spring and summer when plants are flowering and many animals are breeding. In the winter, some animals, such as frogs, hibernate, but it's a good time to see birds.

Early morning and dusk are particularly good times to spot birds, voles, bats and other small mammals.

WHERE TO LOOK
Freshwater life can be found in lakes, ponds (in parks and gardens), ditches and canals. You may even find plants and insects in rainwater tubs.

Many small water animals live among plants growing near the bank. Birds often build nests here, too. Other animals swim in open water.

If a pond or stream is not too shaded or polluted it can have many plants and animals. Here are some places to look for them.

Look on the surface for insects, birds and plants.

Look among reeds for birds' nests, but don't touch them.

Some plants grow completely submerged in water.

Snails live on plants at the bottom.

A lot of plants grow on the bank or in shallow water near the bank. Others grow in deeper water. They may be rooted in the bottom but have leaves floating on the water surface, or they may float freely in open water. The plants in this book have been divided into groups according to where they usually grow.

TAKE CARE
Plants and animals live in harmony with each other and their surroundings (see page 54). If you remove them you will upset the balance.

Look along banks for flowers, reeds and grasses.

Look for holes in the bank where animals live.

Some insects, such as Pond Skaters, skim over the surface.

Some animals swim in open water.

WHAT TO TAKE SPOTTING

When you go out spotting, take the following items with you:

- this book;
- a magnifying glass;
- a clear plastic ruler for measuring what you find;
- binoculars, if you have them, for bird watching;
- a notebook and pencil to draw pictures of the things you find and to make notes about when and where you see them.

DO NOT DISTURB
When you go out spotting be as quiet as possible. It is important not to frighten or disturb any of the wildlife you find in and around ponds and lakes. For example, it is illegal to disturb breeding birds, their nests or their eggs.

Make sure you don't touch any of the animals you are trying to identify, or pick any wild flowers.

AN UNDERWATER VIEWER

To make a viewer for watching underwater life, you could use a large, clear plastic tub or a glass bowl. Hold the viewer just under the water's surface and look in through the open end.

An underwater viewer

MEASURING PLANTS AND ANIMALS

The plants and animals in this book are not drawn to scale, but the average size of each species is given in the description beside it. The measurements are given in millimetres (mm), centimetres (cm) or metres (m) and the pictures below show you how they are measured.

Plants – height from ground or water-level or width of flowerhead

Bats, moths and dragonflies – distance across wingspan

Terrapins and molluscs – height or length of shell

Mammals, frogs and toads – body length, not including tail

Birds, fishes, reptiles, newts, salamanders, spiders and insects – total body length (including tail but not legs)

BANKSIDE PLANTS

Tree in winter

Finely-toothed leaves of the White Willow

Catkin

↑ WHITE WILLOW
Often cut back to produce lots of shoots for basket-making. Common near water. Silky hairs on leaves make them look white. Catkins in April and May. Up to 20m tall.

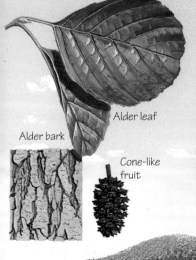

Alder leaf

Alder bark

Cone-like fruit

Tree in winter

↑ COMMON ALDER
Small tree, common beside ponds and lakes and in swampy areas. Fruits look like woody cones. Rounded leaves with notched tips. Reddish catkins in April. Up to 12m tall.

BANKSIDE PLANTS

The months specified at the end of each description tell you when you will see these plants in flower.

Underside of leaf

↑ COMMON OSIER
Shrub found beside water and in hedgerows. Twigs are used to make baskets. Leaves are glossy green on top and silvery-white below. Up to 5m tall. Catkins around April.

Catkin

← MARSH MARIGOLD
Also called the Kingcup. Belongs to the Buttercup family. Found growing in marshy places. Up to 45cm tall. May.

➡ WATER FORGET-ME-NOT
Grows in damp shady places next to still or running water. Blue flowers that may be pink at first. Flowers about 1cm across. June-Oct.

SHALLOW-WATER PLANTS

← YELLOW FLAG IRIS
Common in marshes and
in shallow running or still
water. Yellow flowers
about 8mm across. About
1m tall. May-July.

Fruits

→ WATER PLANTAIN
Grows beside ponds, lakes,
canals and slow rivers. Large,
pointed, oval leaves. Pink or
white flowers with three
petals. Flowers about 8mm
across. Up to 1m tall. July-Aug.

← GREAT WILLOWHERB
Also known as Codlins-
and-cream. Found
growing in marshy places.
Leaves are hairy. About 1m
tall. Flowers about 25mm
across. July-Aug.

13

SHALLOW-WATER PLANTS

➡ MEADOWSWEET
Large clusters of tiny, cream-coloured, sweet-scented flowers. In water meadows, beside ditches and rivers. Up to 80cm tall. May-Sept.

Undersides of leaves are silvery-grey

◀ FLOWERING RUSH
Long, rush-like leaves. Main flower stem topped by a cluster of about 20 narrow-stemmed pink flowers. Marshy areas. About 1m tall. June-Aug.

➡ COMMON BULRUSH
Spreads out into the water from the banks. Stout, rounded stems are full of pulp. Flowers grow in tightly packed bunches. Up to 3m tall.

Bunches of flowers

← COMMON REED

Forms dense reedbeds in fenlands and around pond and lake edges. Brownish flowers grow in tufts about 30cm long. Woody stems often over 4m tall.

Male flowers

Fruits

→ BUR-REED

Seeds are eaten by wild birds. Grows in clumps in shallow water. Long, flat leaves. Male flowers at tips of stems, spiky fruits lower down. Up to 1.5m tall. July-Aug.

Seedhead

Flowering head

← GREAT REEDMACE

Often wrongly called a Bulrush. Tall, pointed leaves. Seeds packed in dark brown, velvety seedhead at the ends of spiky stems. Marshy ground by still or slow-moving water. Up to 2.5m tall. June-Aug.

FLOATING-LEAVED PLANTS

← WATER CROWFOOT
Common in lowland parts of Britain. Most of the plant is underwater, but flowers cover the surface of ponds and streams in May and June. Rooted in mud on the bottom. Flowers 1-2cm across.

Floating leaves

→ FROGBIT
Spreads across ponds and canals by putting out runners. Undersides of the leaves shelter many water animals. Flowers about 2.5cm across. July-Aug.

Runner

Seedhead

← YELLOW WATER-LILY
Glossy floating leaves look like blunt, rounded arrowheads. Seedheads shaped like wine carafes. Yellow flowers abou 7cm across. June-Aug.

← WHITE WATER-LILY
Flowers and leaves float on the surface of the water White petals, sometimes tinged with pink. Flowers up to 20cm across. June-Aug.

FLOATING-LEAVED AND FLOATING PLANTS

➡ BROAD-LEAVED PONDWEED

Common in shallow pools of acid water. Oval floating leaves and thin, delicate underwater leaves. Spikes of green flowers. Up to 1m tall. June-Aug.

Floating leaves

⬅ ARROWHEAD

Long, narrow underwater leaves grow in spring, followed by oval floating leaves and large upper leaves like arrowheads. In muddy water. Up to 1m tall. June-Aug.

⬆ LESSER DUCKWEED

Tiny free-floating plant. Often carpets entire pond surface. Eaten by fishes and ducks. 5-6mm across.

➡ WATER SOLDIER

Remains underwater except when it flowers (May-Aug). Sharp, sword-like leaves stand above the water surface. Sinks after flowering. Up to 25cm above water.

Saw-edged leaves

UNDERWATER PLANTS

➡ CANADIAN PONDWEED
Introduced into Europe in about 1850. Grows fast and has choked many waterways. Leaves grow in threes on stem. Flowers are rare. Up to 3.5m long. June-Sept.

Delicate leaves grow underwater

◀ SPIKED WATER MILFOIL
Very common in chalky, still water. Many small invertebrates shelter on the underwater leaves. Slender flower stem grows above water. Up to 3.5m long. June-July.

➡ WATER VIOLET
Long stem and feathery leaves are underwater. Cluster of flowers rises up to 40cm above the water. Rare. Found in ditches, ponds and lakes. Mainly eastern Britain. May-June.

Water surface

Underwater view

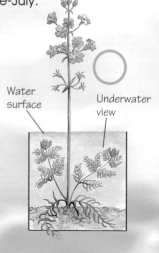

← MARE'S TAIL
Narrow leaves, grouped in whorls around stem. Tiny flowers appear at base of leaves. Grows partly submerged in still or slow-moving water. Up to 1m tall. June-July.

Star-shaped cluster of leaves

→ WATER STARWORT
This water weed is often seen in ditches, streams and ponds. Upper leaves float on the surface in star-shaped clusters. Very small flowers at base of the leaves. Up to 50cm long. May-Sept.

Tiny flowers

Anchored to the mud by colourless threads

← STONEWORT
This plant does not have flowers. It is found in chalky or salty water. It is brittle and snaps easily. Eaten by ducks. Up to 20cm long.

19

DUCKS

Female

Male

← MALLARD
Common all year round. Only the female, or duck, gives the familiar, loud "quack". Upends to catch tiny water animals and plants. Builds a nest on the bank. 58cm long.

➡TEAL
Smallest European duck. Breeds in Britain. Also gathers here in large flocks in winter. Can take off vertically from the water. A very shy bird. 35cm long.

Female

Male

Male

Female

← GOLDENEYE
A sea duck. Visits lakes, coasts and reservoirs in winter. Frequently dives to catch small water animals. Name comes from its bright golden eyes. 46cm long.

Long bill

◀ SHOVELER

Often seen in marshy places. Eats mainly water weeds, which it filters through its long flat bill. Also eats small flying insects. Sits low in the water. 51cm long.

Female

Male

Female

Male

▲ POCHARD

Most likely to be seen in winter. Many fly to Europe to breed. Dives for food. Like the Tufted Duck, it runs across the water before taking off. 46cm long.

Pochard ducklings following their mother

◀ TUFTED DUCK

Common on all kinds of ponds and lakes. Nests close to the water.
Another diving duck, it eats water weeds and small water animals, such as pond snails. 43cm long.

Female

Male

21

GREBES, SWAN

The young are stripy

Winter

Summer

◀ GREAT CRESTED GREBE
Seen on reservoirs and large lakes. Swims well. Dives for fish. Elaborate, noisy courtship displays in spring. Nests on platforms of vegetation moored to reeds. 48cm long.

Winter

Summer

⬇ MUTE SWAN
Most common British swan. Nests on huge platforms of reeds in shallow water or on banks. Listen for the strange creaking noise it makes in flight. Eats grass, weeds, insects and molluscs. 152cm long.

⬆ LITTLE GREBE or DABCHICK
An expert swimmer, it dives to escape danger and to fish. Some are eaten by Pike. Nests in dense cover on heaps of vegetation. Shy and hard to spot. 27cm long.

Long neck helps it feed in deep water

Cygnet (young swan)

HERON, GULL, BITTERN

➡ GREY HERON
Prefers marshy places.
Stands still for long periods
in shallow water. Nests in
colonies in trees. Eats fishes,
frogs, small mammals and
young birds. 92cm long.

Heron nestling in
tree-top nest

Winter

Summer

◀ BLACK-HEADED GULL
Common in winter.
Prefers swampy lakes.
Likes to nest on floating
islands of vegetation.
Scavenges in dockyards,
on rubbish dumps. Eats
insects and worms. 37cm long.

Dark brown head
in summer only

➡ BITTERN
Rare. Found in East Anglian
fens. "Freezes" with bill vertical
when alarmed, making its
striped body blend with the
reeds around it. The male's
call is an eerie carrying
"boom". 75cm long.

RAILS

← WATER RAIL
Skulks among the waterside plants, often in fenland. Secretive. Rarely flies, but can swim. Has a high, piglet-like squeal. Eats seeds, plants and snails. 28cm long.

Head jerks forward with each step

← MOORHEN
Very common on all inland waters. Runs for cover if approached. Nests on a high pile of foliage among waterside plants. Young are brown. 33cm long.

↓ COOT
Likes large lakes. Dives for water plants or grazes on land. Nest is similar to the Moorhen's, but in deeper water. Young are grey. 38cm long.

Coot's nest anchored to reeds

OSPREY, WARBLER, KINGFISHER

Upper parts are dark brown

➡ OSPREY

Breeds on a few Scottish lochs. Rare. Swoops down to the water surface and seizes big fishes with its sharp talons. Nests high in trees, usually in pines. 66cm long.

➡ REED WARBLER

Summer visitor. Weaves a nest around reeds growing in shallow water. Its call is a continuous "churring" noise. Eats insects. 13cm long.

Reed Warbler's young in nest

➡ KINGFISHER

Usually lives near running water, but may be seen by ponds or lakes. Nests in a hole tunnelled in soft earth in the bank. Dives from a perch to catch fishes. 17cm long.

Listen for its shrill whistle

MINK, OTTER, SHREW

◀ EUROPEAN MINK
Introduced into Britain
this century from the USA.
Bred for its fur. Now lives
wild in large numbers.
A good swimmer.
Catches fishes,
small mammals,
frogs and birds.
About 40cm long.

*Feet are
slightly webbed*

⬇ OTTER
Shy and nocturnal, often
seen near rivers, but
sometimes near lakes.
Becoming rare. An
expert swimmer.
Eats fishes, frogs,
crayfish, birds and
mammals. About
70cm long.

➡ WATER SHREW
Often seen near slow streams,
but may be seen near still
water with dense cover.
Swims well. Walks along
the bottom hunting
water animals. Its saliva
is poisonous. About
8cm long.

*Makes loud
whistling noises*

BAT, RAT, VOLE

➡ DAUBENTON'S or WATER BAT

Lives mainly in woods, often near water. Flies over water surface and catches Mayflies and other insects. Hunts by day or by night. About 40cm long. Wing span 24cm.

Flies very fast and very low

⬅ COMMON RAT

May be seen swimming in lakes, rivers and ponds. Eats anything. Scavenges mainly at night. Lives in a burrow in the bank. Up to 26cm long. Tail up to 23cm long.

Coat may also be black

➡ WATER VOLE

Often wrongly called the Water Rat. Swims well, diving head-first from the bank. Eats mainly plants but also worms, snails and fishes. Up to 22cm long. Tail 10-14cm long.

Listen for the "plop" it makes diving into the water

27

TROUT, CHARR, STICKLEBACK, PIKE

Brown Trout

Always spotted, but colour varies

Charr

🔺 BROWN TROUT

Likes lakes with fast-flowing water. Feeds on snails, crustaceans and insects. Large ones eat other fishes. Young are called parr. 50cm long.

🔺 CHARR

Lives in mountain lakes in Britain, in rivers and seas in northern Europe. In rivers they grow to 1m long; in lakes they only reach 25cm.

Three spines

Male in breeding colours

🔻 PIKE

Prefers clean water with lots of plants. Lurks among weeds, preying on frogs and fishes, sometimes birds or mammals too. Up to 1.3m long.

🔺 STICKLEBACK

Males make nests in the sand with weeds, then guard the eggs and the young. Found in rivers, ponds, lakes and shallow seas. Eats crustaceans. Up to 6cm long.

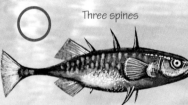

RUDD, TENCH, MINNOW, WEATHERFISH

➡ RUDD
Seen in weedy ponds and lakes. Often so many breed that food becomes scarce and they remain small. Feeds mainly on insects near the surface. 40cm long.

⬅ TENCH
Lives among weeds at the bottom of ponds and lakes. Can survive harsh winters buried in the mud. Eats plants and small water animals. 50cm long.

➡ WEATHERFISH
Can live in stagnant water. Comes to surface to breathe. Restless during thundery weather. Not in Britain. 15cm long.

⬇ MINNOW
Often seen in fast-moving schools in lakes, streams and rivers. Eaten by water birds and other fishes. Eats small water animals. 8cm long.

Male in breeding colours

PERCH, GUDGEON, GOLDFISH

⬆ PERCH
Likes clean, shady water.
Lurks under bridges and
overhanging trees. Feeds
on smaller fishes, water
insect larvae and
crustaceans. 15-30cm long.

⬇ GUDGEON
A bottom-dweller. Feeds
on worms, snails, insect
larvae and crustaceans.
Breaks up its food using
teeth in its throat.
15cm long.

Barbel

⬅ GOLDFISH
Originally from
China and Japan,
now widespread
in Europe. Likes
weedy bottoms
of lakes and slow rivers.
Eats worms and
custaceans. 30cm long.

*Goldfishes are this
dull colour in the wild*

CARP, WELS

➡ CARP
Likes warm,
weedy lakes.
Basks near
the surface in
sunny weather.
Eats mainly plants.
Also sucks up mud
and sifts out tiny animals.
61cm long.

Barbels

Grinds up
food with
teeth in
its throat

⬆ CRUCIAN CARP
Widespread in still pools
and lakes in southern
England. Prefers densely
weeded water. Lays eggs
on water plants in early
summer. 51cm long.

⬇ WELS
The only native European
catfish. Introduced into
Britain this century. Rare.
Active mainly at night.
Eats fishes, frogs, water
mammals and water
birds. 3m long.

Barbels

BREAM, ROACH, BITTERLING, EEL

Sliver Bream

← SILVER BREAM
Found in small groups
close to the bottom.
Feeds on water insect
larvae. Lays its eggs
among water plants.
15cm long.

Roach

↑ ROACH
Widespread in lowland
lakes and rivers in Britain.
Forms large schools at
spawning time (April-May).
Eats snails, insect larvae and
crustaceans. 50cm long.

↓ BITTERLING
Likes weedy lowland waters.
Not in Britain. The female lay
eggs inside a mussel's shell.
The mussel later releases the
baby fish, which stick to
their mother's side until
they mature. 9cm long.

↓ EEL
Spawned in mid-Atlantic,
then travels to Europe.
The elver (young eel) swims
upstream to ponds and
lakes. After many years, it
returns to the Atlantic to
breed and die.
About 1m long.

Female

Egg-laying
tube

Mussel

Can travel over land

TOADS

Toads look more squat than frogs, and have drier, warty skin. Toads hibernate on land and are often seen far from water.

◀ COMMON TOAD
Can swim, but goes into the water only to breed. Hunts after dusk, catching snails, worms and insects. Sheds its skin in summer. Female up to 13cm long, male smaller.

Male

Tadpole

Long strings of toadspawn

➡ NATTERJACK TOAD
Becoming rare in Britain. Seen only in the breeding season. The male has a very loud croak. Catches insects at night. Usually 7-8cm long.

Water surface

◀ YELLOW-BELLIED TOAD
Lives in water all year round. May be seen in puddles as well as in ponds and lakes. Central and southern parts of Europe, but not in Britain. Eats small insects. Up to 5cm long.

33

FROGS

➡ **COMMON FROG**
Found in damp, shady places. Mates and lays its eggs in water. Hibernates in mud at the bottom of ponds and lakes. Eats slugs, insects, worms and snails. Up to 10cm long.

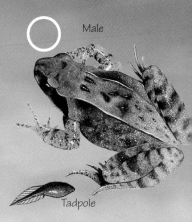
Male

Tadpole

Mass of frogspawn

⬅ **MARSH FROG**
Introduced into Britain from Europe. Swallows newts, fishes, frogs and small mammals whole. The male makes a very loud croak at spawning time. About 15cm long.

➡ **EDIBLE FROG**
Spends a lot of time in water, but may be seen sunning itself on land. Not in Britain. Its legs are eaten as a delicacy. Up to 12cm long.

⬅ **PARSLEY FROG**
A good swimmer. Its croak sounds like squeaky shoes. Not in Britain. Eats small invertebrates. About 5cm long.

➡ EUROPEAN TREE FROG

Climbs low trees and bushes, and can catch flying insects in mid-air. Breeds in water with dense cover. Croaks in rainy weather. Not in Britain. Up to 5cm long.

Clings with sucker pads on the toes

⬅ **AGILE FROG**

Likes fields and open woodland. Has very long hind legs and jumps well. Eats molluscs and small insects. Not in Britain. Up to 9cm long.

The pictures below show the stages tadpoles go through before they become adult frogs or toads. Frogs, toads and newts usually spend most of their lives on land, but they all return to the water to mate and lay their eggs.

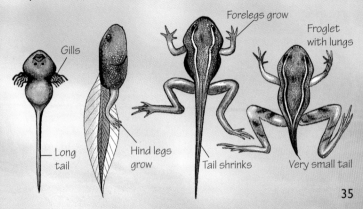

Gills

Long tail

Hind legs grow

Forelegs grow

Tail shrinks

Froglet with lungs

Very small tail

NEWTS

Crest only at breeding time

Male

Tadpole

Female

Eggs on water plants

⬆ SMOOTH NEWT
Spends autumn and winter on land, and mates and lays eggs in water in the spring. Common in lowland parts of Britain. Eats tadpoles, snails and insects. 11cm long.

➡ ALPINE NEWT
Found mainly in mountainous, wooded country. Not in Britain. Young newt can grow a new limb if it loses one. Eats worms, snails, insects and crustaceans. 12cm long.

Male

Low crest at breeding time

Male has a high spiky crest at breeding time

⬅ GREAT CRESTED NEWT
Also known as a Warty Newt. Spends a lot of time in ponds. Glands in its skin produce a sticky fluid that repels predators. 14cm long.

NEWT, SALAMANDER, TERRAPIN

Male

◀ PALMATE NEWT
Prefers shallow water. Male has webbed toes and a thread-like extension to its tail. Eats mainly insects, worms and insect larvae. Not in Ireland. 9cm long.

Webbed toes

Tail filament

➡ SALAMANDER
Usually found near water, but hibernates under stones and in other dry places. Lays eggs in water. Eats slugs and worms. Active mainly at night. Not in Britain. 20cm long.

Colour patterns vary

⬇ EUROPEAN POND TERRAPIN
Found in ponds and marshy places. Always eats its food in water. Hibernates and lays its eggs in mud. Hunts frogs, newts, fishes. Not in Britain. Shell up to 20cm long.

Hunts in water and on land

SNAKES

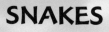

Grass Snakes have a yellow "collar" edged in black

⬅ GRASS SNAKE
Harmless snake found near water and in dry places. Can stay underwater for a long time. A good hunter. Swallows frogs alive. Not found in Ireland. Up to 120cm long.

Eggs are about 3cm long

➡ VIPERINE SNAKE
Seen in or near weedy ponds, streams and ditches. Swallows fishes whole. Also eats frogs, worms and sometimes newts and toads. Not found in Britain. Up to 70cm long.

Colour and pattern varies

Dark blotches on the sides

Pattern varies greatly

⬅ DICE SNAKE
An expert swimmer, hunts or lies in wait for fish, often near the bottom in deep water. Spends the winter on land. Not found in Britain. Up to 75cm long.

BEETLES

➡ GREAT SILVER WATER BEETLE

Looks silvery because of the air bubble it carries on its body. Eats mainly plants, but larva eats small animals. Rare. Likes weedy ponds. 37-48mm long.

⬅ GREAT DIVING BEETLE

A fierce predator common in weedy ponds. Rises to the surface to trap air around its body. Larva lives in water. Both eat newts, small fish and tadpoles. 30-35mm long.

Larva

➡ WHIRLIGIG BEETLE

Seen paddling in rapid circles on water surface. Can also fly and dive. Larva lives in water and feeds on tiny animals. Adult eats flies and other insects. 6-8mm long.

⬅ SCREECH BEETLE

Squeaks by rubbing its wing cases and abdomen together if caught. Hunts worms and insect larvae. Larva can breathe in mud. 8-10mm long.

Larva

39

BUGS

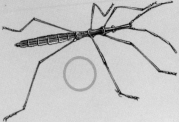

← WATER MEASURER
Often seen near banks
of ponds and slow
streams and rivers.
Winters on the bank.
Eats water insects and
water fleas. 9-12mm long.

→ POND SKATER
Often seen running across
surface of ponds. Jumps
well, sometimes dives.
Picks up dead insects
from the water surface
to eat. 8-10mm long.

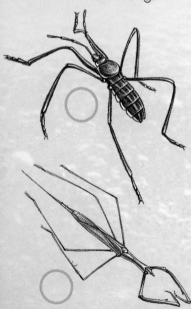

← WATER CRICKET
Skims across surface of
ponds and slow streams.
Can also dive. Lays its
eggs on waterside plants.
Feeds on spiders and
insects. 6-7mm long.

← WATER STICK INSECT
Common near banks of
ponds and lakes. Can fly.
Front feet act like a pair of
scissors and snap shut on
prey. Not related to true
stick insects. 30-35mm long.

➡ WATER SCORPION
Usually sits under water waiting for prey, which it grasps with its forelegs. Eats tadpoles, insects and small fish. Found in ponds and shallow lakes. 18-22mm long.

⬅ LESSER WATER BOATMAN
Swims right way up. Often seen in stagnant water. Rises to the surface to collect air. Feeds on dead animals and plants on the bottom. 12-14mm long.

⬅ SAUCER BUG
Likes still, muddy water. Its mouthparts can give a painful bite. Cannot fly, but swims well. Preys on small water animals, even small fish. 12-16mm long.

➡ WATER BOATMAN
Very common in still water. Swims well, mainly on its back. Uses its hairy hind legs for swimming. Can bite. Eats tadpoles, insects and small fish. 15mm long.

Breathes from tail end

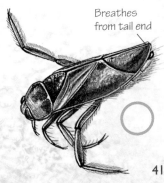

41

DRAGONFLIES

Dragonflies and damselflies lay eggs in water, on plants or on the bottom mud. When a nymph is fully grown, it climbs to the surface. Its skin splits, and an adult emerges.

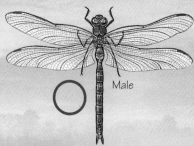

Male

◀ BROWN HAWKER
The female lays eggs on water plants. Common by water. Nymph eats worms, small fish and water fleas. Adult's wingspan about 100mm.

➡ BROAD-BODIED CHASER
Likes ponds with plants. Flies in short bursts. Nymph can survive droughts buried in mud. Adult's wingspan 75mm.

Male

Female

⬇ EMPEROR DRAGONFLY
Seen over ponds and far from water in the summer. Catches flies and butterflies in mid-air. Wingspan 105mm.

Male

Nymph

Female

⬇ DOWNY EMERALD
Fairly common over all kinds of still water in southern England. Also hunts in or near woods at dusk. Like all dragonflies, it can fly backwards. Wingspan 68mm.

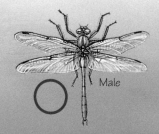

Male

DAMSELFLIES

Damselflies are smaller and more delicate-looking than dragonflies. They rest with their wings folded, not spread out like dragonflies.

➡ EMERALD DAMSELFLY

Usually flies over waterside plants, but may be seen far from water. Male is bright green, female brownish. Wingspan 45-50mm.

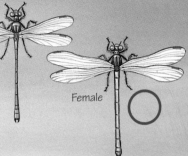

Male

Female

⬅ COMMON ISCHNURA or BLUE-TAILED DAMSELFLY

Very common near still or slow-moving water in the summer. Greenish-black body. Wingspan 35mm.

Male

➡ BANDED DEMOISELLE

Sometimes seen over ponds, but prefers running water. Green, shiny body. Nymph hibernates twice. Adult's wingspan 60-65mm.

Female

Male

⬅ RUDDY DARTER

Seen flying above weedy ponds and ditches in marshy places. Nymph usually changes into an adult at night. Adult's wingspan 55mm.

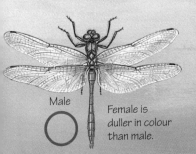

Male

Female is duller in colour than male.

43

DRONE FLY, GNAT, CRANEFLY

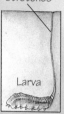

Breathing tube stretches

Larva

← DRONE FLY
Drones like a bee when it flies. Larva (called a "Rat-tailed Maggot") lives in ditches and ponds. Larva up to 20mm long. Adult 15mm long.

Water surface

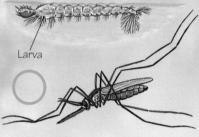

Larva

← SPOTTED GNAT
The female sucks blood and may carry malaria (but not in Britain). Larva lies horizontally just below the surface of ponds with plenty of plants. Adult 6-7mm long.

➡ COMMON GNAT or MOSQUITO
Common near stagnant water. Larvae hang almost vertically below the surface. Eggs float in raft-like clusters. 6-7mm long.

Water surface

Larva called a leatherjacket

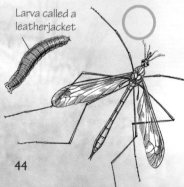

← GIANT CRANEFLY or DADDY-LONG-LEGS
Largest British true fly. Usually found near still water. Swarms at dusk. Larva lives in mud in shallows, eating plant roots. 30-40mm long.

ALDER FLY, CADDIS FLY, MIDGE

➡ ALDER FLY
Commonly seen May-June, crawling over waterside plants. Flies at dusk. Lays eggs on reeds. Larvae live in mud, often in deep rivers. 20mm long.

Egg mat

⬅ CADDIS FLY
Seen flying near water at dusk. Larva lives in water. Many Caddis larvae live in cases made of leaves and twigs. Adult 15-20 mm long.

Caddis larva in case made of leaves

➡ PHANTOM MIDGE
Named after larva's near-transparent body. Larva found floating in still water. Adults sometimes fly in big swarms near lakes. Larva 5-10mm long Adult about 6mm long.

Larva

MOTH, MAYFLY, SPRINGTAIL

◄ CHINA-MARK MOTH
Eggs are laid on floating leaves. Larvae hibernate and pupate in cases they make from pieces of leaf. Adult flies out of the water in June. Larva up to 20mm long. Adult's wingspan about 30mm.

Larva in leaf case

➡ MAYFLY
Spends most of its life as a nymph on river and lake bottoms. Adult dies shortly after emerging to mate and lay its eggs. Larvae feed mainly on algae scraped off water plants. 40mm long.

Three tails

◄ WATER SPRINGTAIL
Seen on the surface of ponds and lakes. Can make spectacular jumps by flicking down its tail (usually folded beneath its body). Probably eats tiny scraps of dead matter. About 20mm long.

Forked tail

46

MOTH, MITE, SPIDER

➡ BULRUSH WAINSCOT MOTH
Seen in late summer near reedbeds. The female lays eggs inside reedmace stems. Larvae feed on the pith and pupate inside the stem. Adult's wingspan 45-50mm.

Pupa inside stem of reedmace

Joints of the legs are hairy

⬅ WATER MITE
Common in all parts of ponds. Larvae suck body fluids of water bugs. Adult eats tiny water animals. About 2mm long.

"Diving bell" attached to water plants

➡ WATER SPIDER
Spends its whole life in a "diving bell", an underwater web filled with air. Preys on insect larvae, tadpoles and small fish. 10-15mm long.

MUSSELS, COCKLE, LIMPET

➡ SWAN MUSSEL
It filters oxygen dissolved in the water and eats algae and tiny animals. Found at the bottom of ponds, canals and lakes. Shell 15-23cm long.

Close-up of larva

⬅ ZEBRA MUSSEL
Found in reservoirs, canals and lakes. Clings to under-water landing stages and stones. Mussel larvae stick to fish until they become adults. Shell 4cm long.

➡ LAKE LIMPET
Found on plant stems and leaves near the edges of ponds and lakes. Also on the undersides of water-lily leaves. Eats algae and tiny weeds. Shell 5cm long.

Seen from above

Side view

⬅ ORB-SHELL COCKLE
Tiny mollusc found on stems of water plants and in bottom mud. Produces tiny live young, not eggs. Adult's shell 8-10mm long.

SNAILS

Jelly-like egg mass

← GREAT POND SNAIL
Crawls over waterside plants, often in stagnant water. Eats small fish and newts. Also eats algae and rotting animal matter. Shell about 5cm long.

→ MARSH SNAIL
Seen in ditches and marshes. Rasps algae off plants with its "radula", a tongue-like organ in its mouth. Shell 3cm long.

Shell opening is ear-shaped

← EAR POND SNAIL
Likes still, weedy water. Glides over surfaces on a layer of slime from its foot. Shell about 4cm long.

→ DWARF POND SNAIL
Can survive long spells of drought buried in mud. Likes ponds, ditches and springs. Shell about 1cm long.

SNAILS

◀ WANDERING SNAIL
The most common Pond snail, found in both still and slow-moving water. Shape of the shell varies. Shell about 2cm long.

Coiled shell, shaped like a ram's horn.

➡ GREAT RAMSHORN SNAIL
Found in all kinds of water, even very stagnant water. Eats algae and rotting matter on the bottom mud. The largest Ramshorn snail. Shell about 3cm long.

◀ MOSS BLADDER SNAIL
Fairly common in ditches and edges of ponds and lakes rich in weeds. Has a shiny, transparent shell and dark body. Shell about 1cm long.

LEECHES, WORMS

➡ HORSE LEECH
Does not suck horses' or any other animals' blood. Swallows whole worms, snails and insects. Swims gracefully. Likes ponds and ditches. Up to 9cm long.

Leeches swim by expanding and contracting their bodies

➡ MEDICINAL LEECH
Formerly used by doctors to bleed people. Ponds. Rare. Young attack small animals (e.g. newts), but adults suck blood from people and other large mammals. Up to about 9cm long.

Teeth make a Y-shaped bite

◀ FLATWORM
Lives in ponds and rivers, under stones or leaves. Scavenges dead matter from the bottom. Also feeds on algae. About 1cm long.

➡ TUBIFEX WORM
Lives in colonies in mud, often in polluted water. Front end is buried in a burrow, tail waves about to get oxygen. Bolts down the burrow if disturbed. Filters food from the mud. About 3cm long.

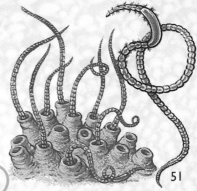

51

TINY WATER ANIMALS

➡ CYCLOPS
Named after a one-eyed monster of Greek legend. Seen in most kinds of still water. Grasps tiny particles of food that float past. The female carries big egg masses. 2-3mm long.

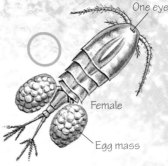

One eye

Female

Egg mass

◀ TRIOPS
Very rare in Britain, but occasionally found in muddy temporary pools. Its eggs can survive if its home dries up. Eats extremely small water animals. About 5cm long.

➡ FAIRY SHRIMP
Usually swims on its back. Found in small ponds and temporary shallow pools. Its eggs can survive if its home dries up. Rare. About 25mm long.

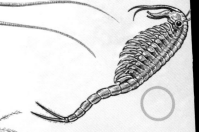

◀ WATER FLEA or DAPHNIA
A crustacean that moves in jerks, like a flea hopping. Lives in open water. Eats algae and tiny water animals. Up to 4mm long.

Tentacle

GREEN HYDRA
Found on water plants, often the undersides of water-lily leaves. Moves by loops or somersaults. Its tentacles have cells that sting and paralyse prey. Up to 2cm long.

Contracts into a blob if disturbed

➡ WATER LOUSE
Found crawling over water plants and on pond bottoms, eating algae and rotting matter. Up to 25mm long.

Cilia

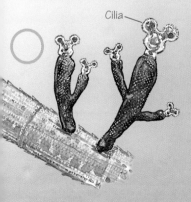

◀ ROTIFER
Some species (like this one) are fixed to water plants. Others swim freely. Rotifers have "cilia" (whirring threads) that draw food towards their mouths. Cilia help some species to swim. 1-2mm long.

LIVING TOGETHER

This book contains only a small selection of the different kinds of wildlife that live in ponds or lakes. To ensure this variety, there has to be enough food and oxygen for all the plants and animals to survive.

This picture shows an example of a food chain. The plants and tiny animals at the bottom of the chain indirectly support the larger animals at the top. Food chains rely on a balance of different kinds of animals and plants. It's important not to disturb this balance.

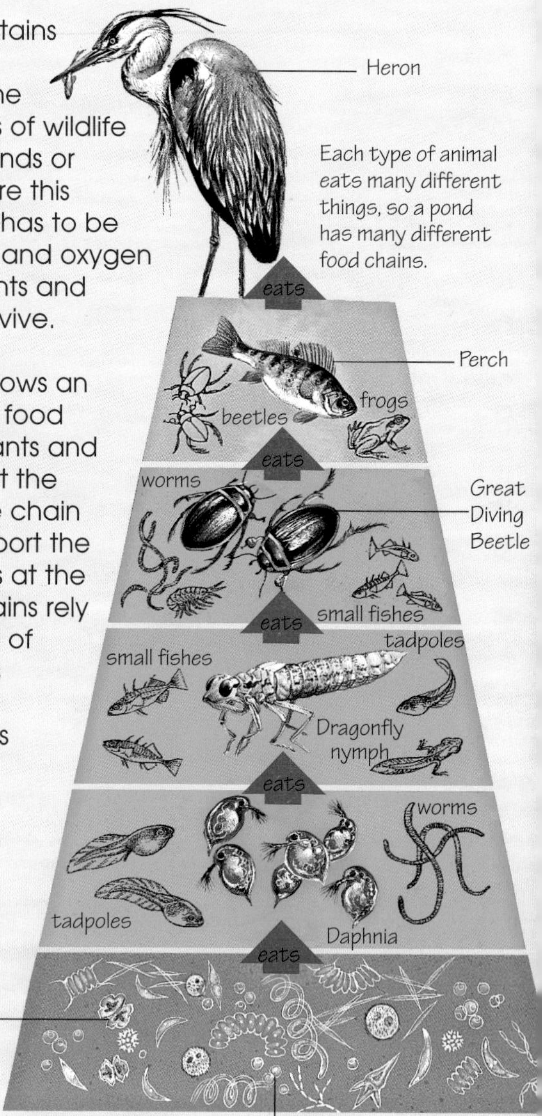

Heron

Each type of animal eats many different things, so a pond has many different food chains.

eats

Perch

beetles   frogs

eats

worms

Great Diving Beetle

small fishes

eats

small fishes   tadpoles

Dragonfly nymph

eats

worms

tadpoles

Daphnia

Plants, such as algae, are at the bottom of a food chain.

eats

microscopic algae

CONSERVATION

To make sure that ponds and lakes are a healthy environment for wildlife, they need to be looked after. If they are neglected, they gradually become clogged with vegetation which uses up all the oxygen in the water. Animals, such as frogs, newts and fish, that can't survive without oxygen will die. To maintain a healthy pond, the vegetation will have to be cleared regularly, which means about every three years.

WHAT YOU CAN DO

By joining a society that organizes conservation projects, you can get help conserve local ponds or canals. You might be asked to help clear vegetation, rubbish or silt on the bottom, or to try to stop local industries polluting the water.

These volunteers are clearing rubbish that has been dumped in a pond.

USEFUL WORDS

This glossary explains some of the more difficult words in this book. Words in *italic* text are defined separately in the glossary.

alga (plural: algae) – a simple plant without roots, stems or leaves.

amphibian – an animal with a backbone that usually lives on land but breeds in water.

annelid – a worm or leech with a body divided into segments.

arachnid – an *invertebrate* with a head, a thorax and four pairs of legs, for example spiders and mites.

barbels (of fishes) – sensitive feelers. Fishes use barbels to find food on the bottom.

breeding colours – some male animals' colouring changes in the breeding season, often becoming brighter. This helps them to attract a mate.

carnivore – a meat-eater.

cocoon – the protective, silky case which a *larva* forms around itself.

crustacean – an animal that lives in water, has two pairs of antennae and jointed legs which are forked, for example shrimps and water fleas.

herbivore – a plant-eater.

hibernate – to survive the winter in an inactive state, usually asleep in a hideout.

invertebrate – an animal without a backbone.

larva (plural larvae) – a stage in the development of some animals before they become adults. For example, a caterpillar is the larval stage of a butterfly.

mammal – a warm-blooded animal that suckles its young, for example voles.

metamorphosis – the changes some animals go through before they become adults.

mollusc – an *invertebrate*